D0606899

ADVENTURES WITH A
PARTY
PLATE

ALSO BY HARRY MILGROM

(Other Books of First Science Experiments)

Adventures with a String

Adventures with a Ball

Adventures with a Plastic Bag

Adventures with a Straw

Adventures with a Paper Cup

First Experiments with Gravity

Explorations in Science

Further Explorations in Science

ADVENTURES WITH A PARTY PLATE

FIRST SCIENCE EXPERIMENTS

by
HARRY MILGROM

Illustrated by
GEORGE WILDE

E. P. DUTTON & CO., INC. New York

For Betty

Published simultaneously in Canada by Clarke, Irwin & Company Limited, Toronto and Vancouver.

Library of Congress Catalog Card Number: 68-28889

You can make many discoveries in science with a party plate.

Get a package of round paper plates in a supermarket, or a five-and-ten cents store. Make sure the plates have a rippled border.

How can you find out the shape of your paper plate?

Put a plate upside down on a large sheet of paper. Draw a pencil line around the edge of the plate.

Lift the plate off the paper.

What do you see on the paper?

A CIRCLE.

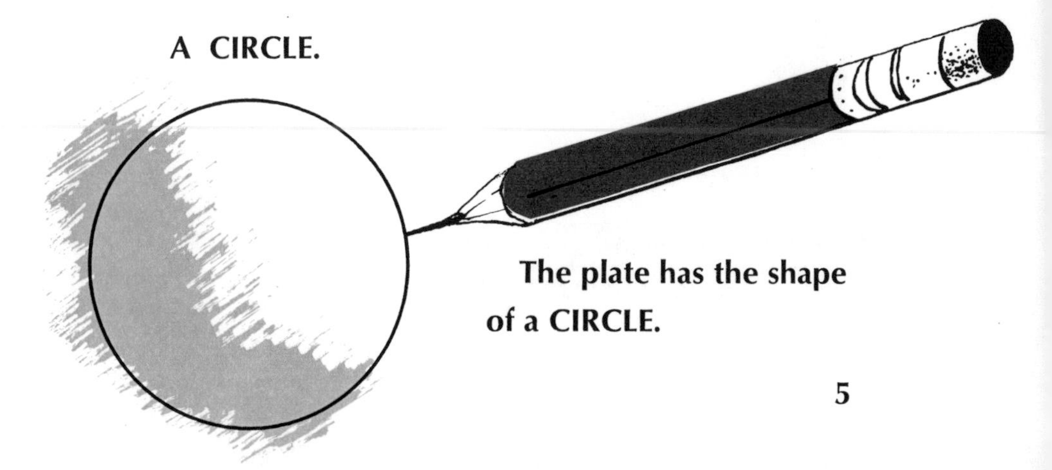

The plate has the shape of a CIRCLE.

What other common things have the shape of a circle?

A penny has the shape of a circle.

A round clock face has the shape of a circle.

A telephone dial has the shape of a circle.

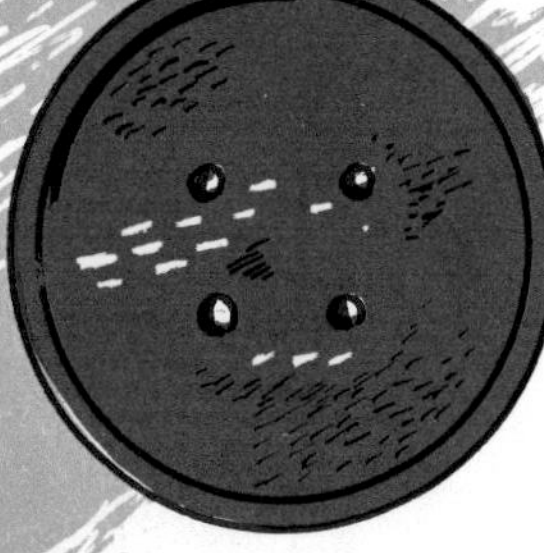

A round button has the shape of a circle.

A checker has the shape of a circle.

What else has the shape of a circle?

How can you find the CENTER of your plate?

Balance the plate upside down on the eraser of a pencil. When the plate is level, the eraser is at the CENTER. With a pencil, make a dot at the CENTER.

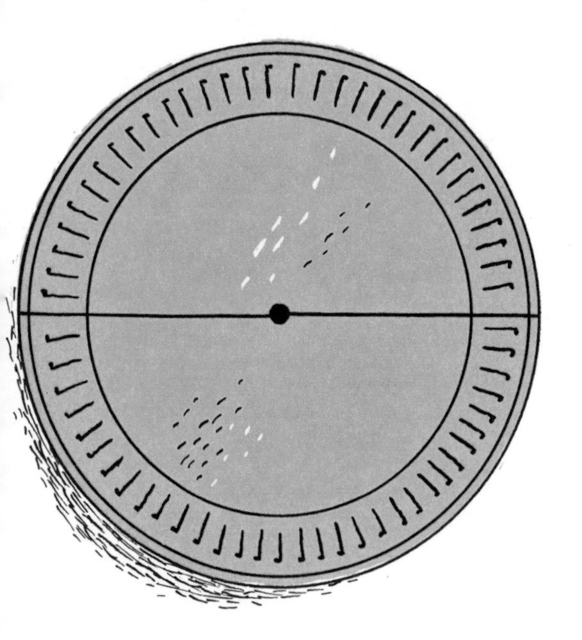

Draw a line that goes from one side of the plate through the dot at the center to the other side. Such a line is called the DIAMETER of the circle.

What is the DIAMETER of your plate?

Is it four inches — six inches — eight inches?

Measure it with a ruler.

Draw a line that goes from the center of the plate to the edge. Such a line is called the RADIUS of the circle.

What is the radius of your plate? Is it half the diameter? Measure it with a ruler.

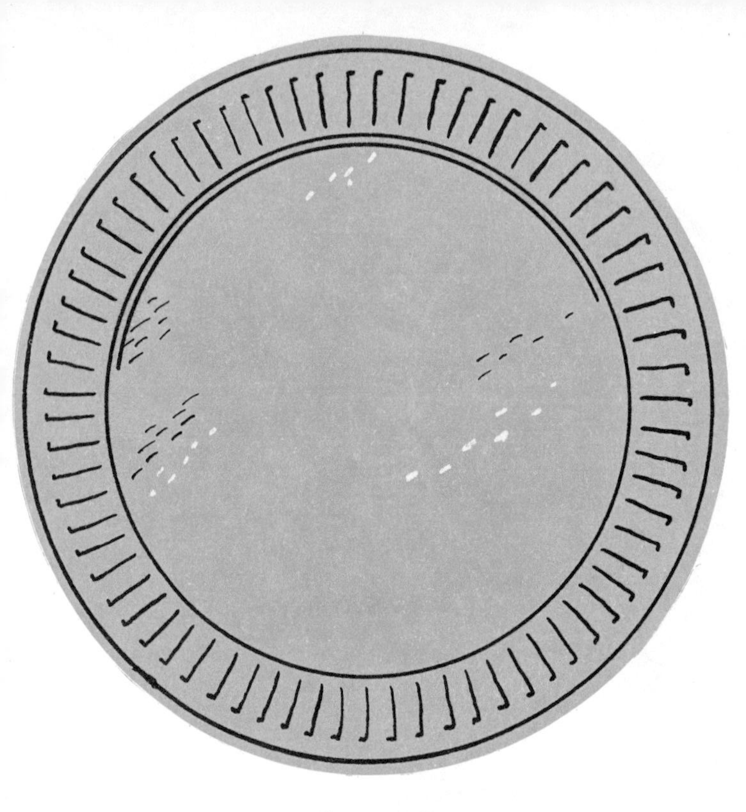

The distance around the edge, or rim, of the plate is called the CIRCUMFERENCE. How can you find the CIRCUMFERENCE of your plate?

Put a dot on the rim. Stand the plate on its rim on the left side of a strip of paper. Make sure the dot is at the bottom.

Put a dot on the paper next to the dot on the plate.

Roll the plate on its rim until the dot reaches the bottom again. Stop. Put another dot on the paper next to the dot on the plate. Measure the distance between the two dots on the strip of paper.

That is the CIRCUMFERENCE of your plate.

Notice that the CIRCUMFERENCE is more than three times the diameter.

A paper plate can help you find out how things fall.

Hold a paper plate in one hand. Hold a penny in the other hand.

Hold both hands up in front of you at the same height. Let go of the plate and the penny at the same time.

What happens?

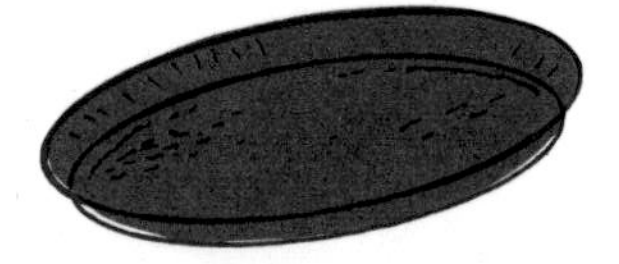

Gravity pulls both things down to the floor.
Which thing lands on the floor first?
The penny lands first.
The plate lands second.

Why does the plate fall more slowly than the penny? The penny is small. Not much air pushes against the penny as it falls. The penny is held back only a little by the air.

The plate is large. Much air pushes against the plate as it falls. The plate is held back by the air. So, the plate falls slowly and lands second.

A parachute is very large. It is held back very much by the air and falls very slowly. That is why a parachute is used to lower things slowly and gently from an airplane to the ground.

From which position will a plate fall with the fewest flip-overs?

Try these positions:

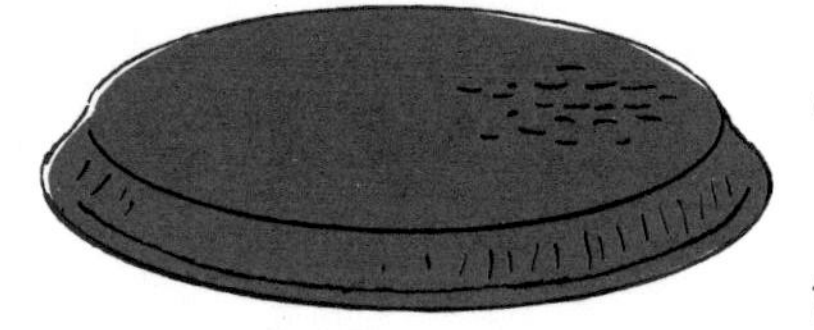

Hold the plate high, upside down. Let go.

How many times does it flip over?

A few times.

Hold the plate high on its side. Let go.
How many times does it flip over?

Many times.

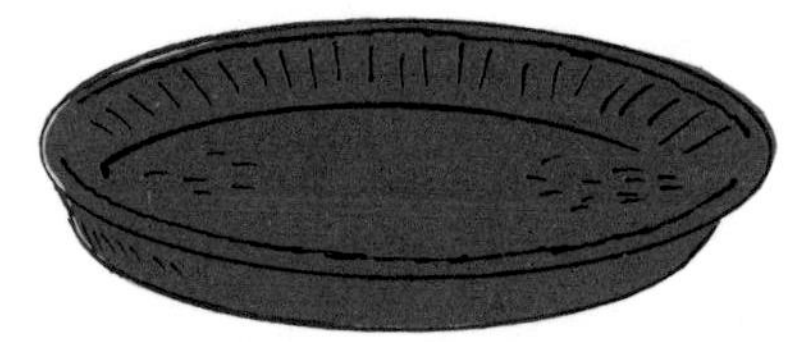

Hold the plate high, right side up. Let go.

How many times does it flip over?

No times.

The plate does not flip over when it falls right side up.

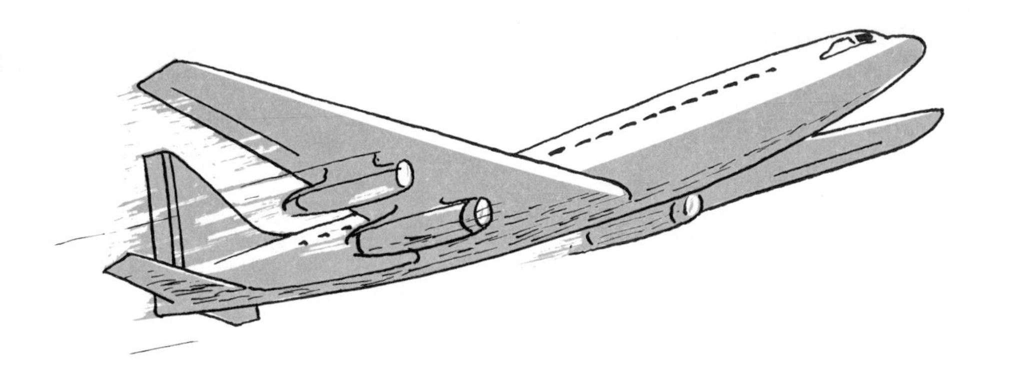

The wings of an airplane are slanted upward like the rim of the plate. That is why an airplane does not flip over as it flies.

How can you make a plate spin around?
One way is to blow it around with air, like this:

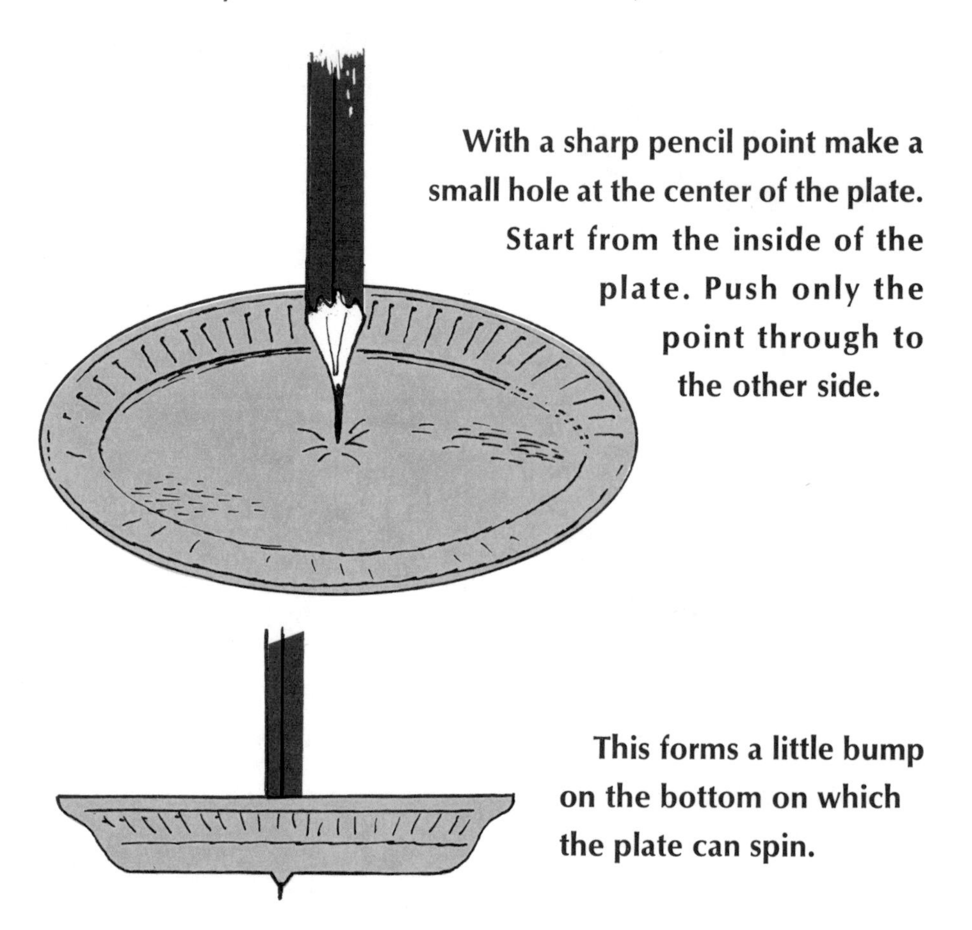

With a sharp pencil point make a small hole at the center of the plate. Start from the inside of the plate. Push only the point through to the other side.

This forms a little bump on the bottom on which the plate can spin.

With a straw, blow air against the ripples on the rim of the plate.

When the air hits the ripples, the plate spins around and around.

A plate that is turned by air can be called an air TURBINE.

In electric power plants, steam is used to spin steam turbines. The steam turbines spin generators which produce electricity.

What is another way to get a plate to spin around?
Find the center of a plate.
Get a pencil about four inches long.

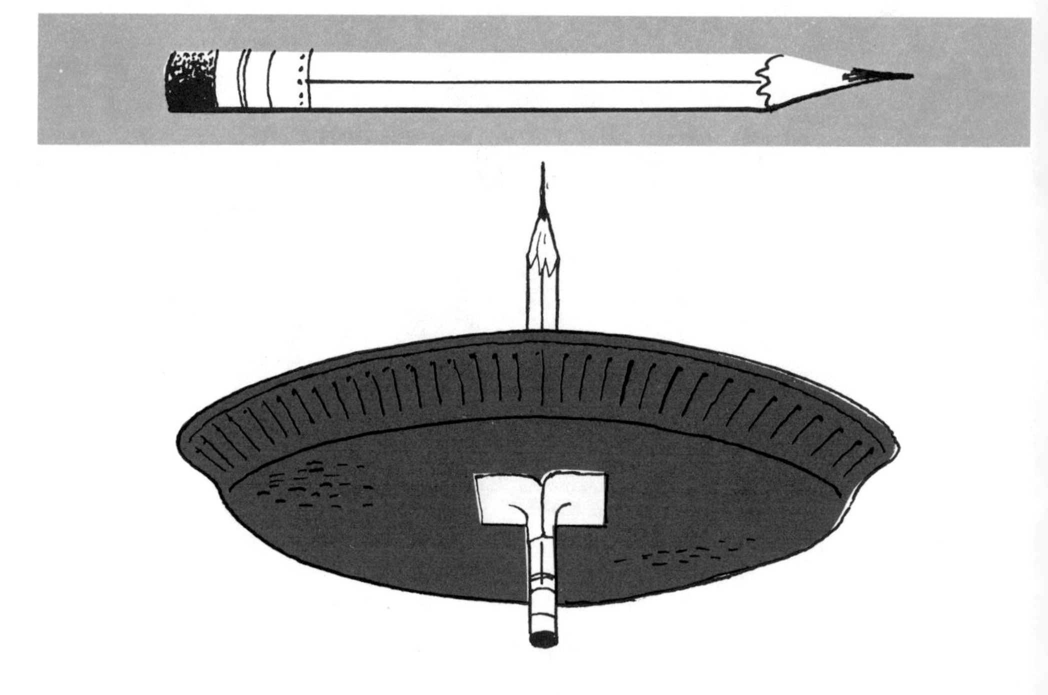

Push the pencil through the center until the eraser is about one inch from the plate.

Tape the pencil to the plate.

Put the eraser end on a smooth table.
Twirl the pencil. What happens?

As long as the plate spins fast, it stands up like a TOP. When the plate begins to slow down, the rim hits the table and the turning stops.

How can you get a plate to roll on its rim without falling down?

Take two plates. Find their centers. Push them together, bottom to bottom.

Push a pencil through the center of each plate. Move one plate to the left side of the pencil. Move the second plate to the right side of the pencil.

Tape the plates to the pencil.

What happens when you try to
roll the two plates and the pencil?

They roll without falling down,
because one plate holds up
the other plate.

The two plates on the pencil are
like WHEELS on an AXLE.

Wheels on axles roll easily.
That is why carriages, wagons,
automobiles, trucks, and trains are
put on wheels and axles.

How can you weigh things with a plate?

Find the center of a plate. With scissors, cut along a radius to the center.

Glue half the plate on a box. Make sure the other half can bend down without rubbing against the box.

Put one penny on the movable part of the plate. What happens?

The plate bends down a little.

Add another penny. What happens?
The plate bends more.
Add another penny. What happens?
The plate bends still more.
The plate is like a SPRING SCALE.
Find out which weighs more — a nickel or a dime.

How can you tell the time of day with a plate? Use the plate to make a SUNDIAL.

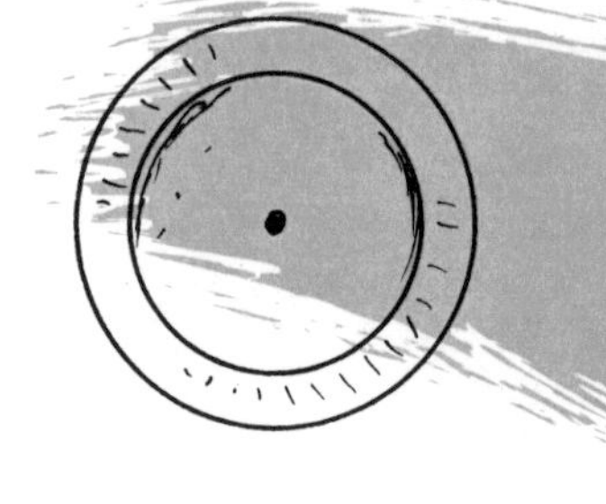

Find the center of the plate.

With scissors, cut a narrow strip from the edge to the center.

Fold the strip back until it is halfway to the uncut part of the plate.

Tape the strip in this position.

Put the plate in sunlight, and point the strip toward the North.

When the shadow of the strip falls to the left, it is morning.

When the shadow falls under the strip, it is noon.

When the shadow falls to the right, it is afternoon.

What time of day does the sundial in the picture show? (Afternoon).

How can you use a plate to show how fast the wind is blowing?

Cut the same kind of a strip in a plate as you cut for the sundial.

This time let the strip stand straight up.

Blow against the strip.
What happens?

A gentle blow bends the strip
a little.

A hard blow bends the strip
a great deal.

The amount of bending shows how
fast the wind is blowing.

How can you use water to make two plates spin around?

Take two plates. Find their centers.

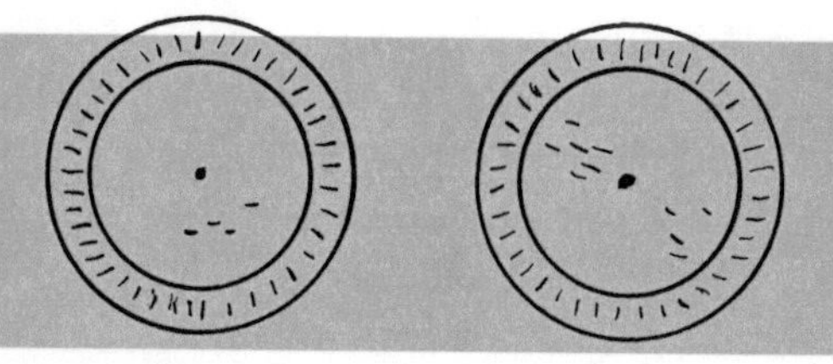

Glue them together, bottom to bottom.

Push a pencil through the centers of the glued plates. Make sure the plates turn easily on the pencil.

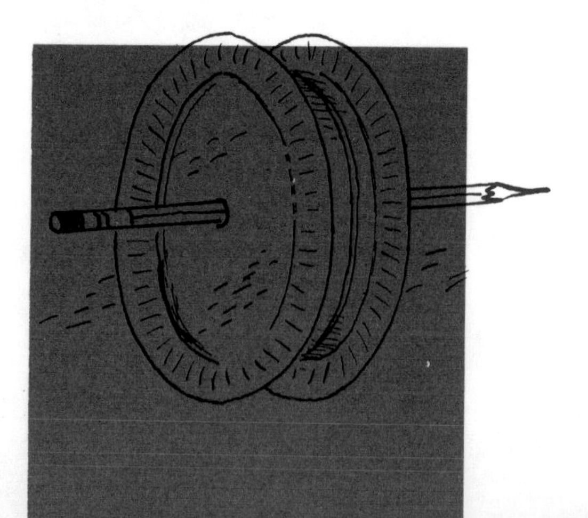

Hold the plates under a faucet and turn on the water.

Let the water fall between the plates at the side. What happens?

The plates spin around as the water falls.

This is a WATER WHEEL.

In hydroelectric power plants, water wheels are turned by falling water. The water wheels spin generators which produce electricity.

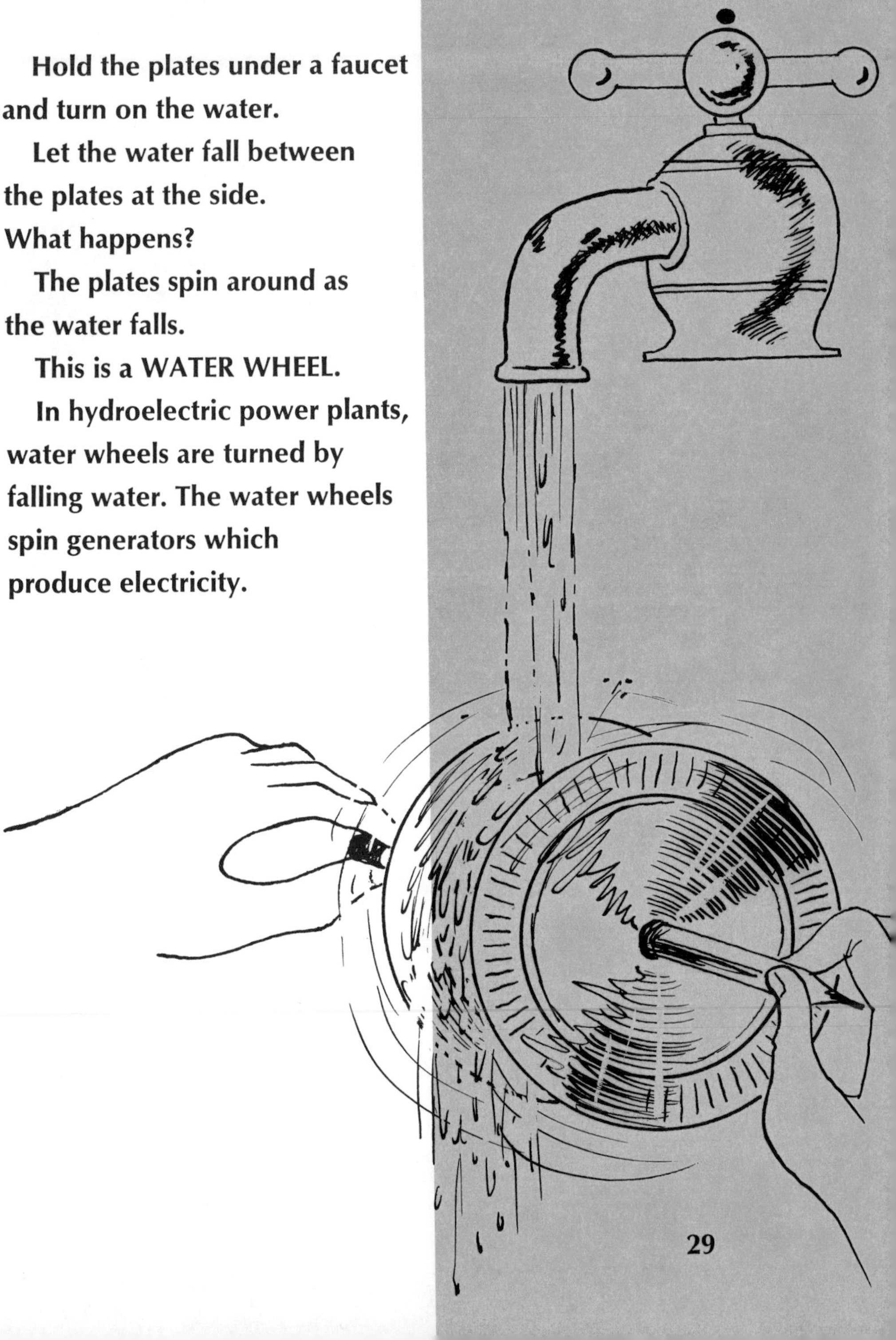

Here are the discoveries you have just made with a party plate.

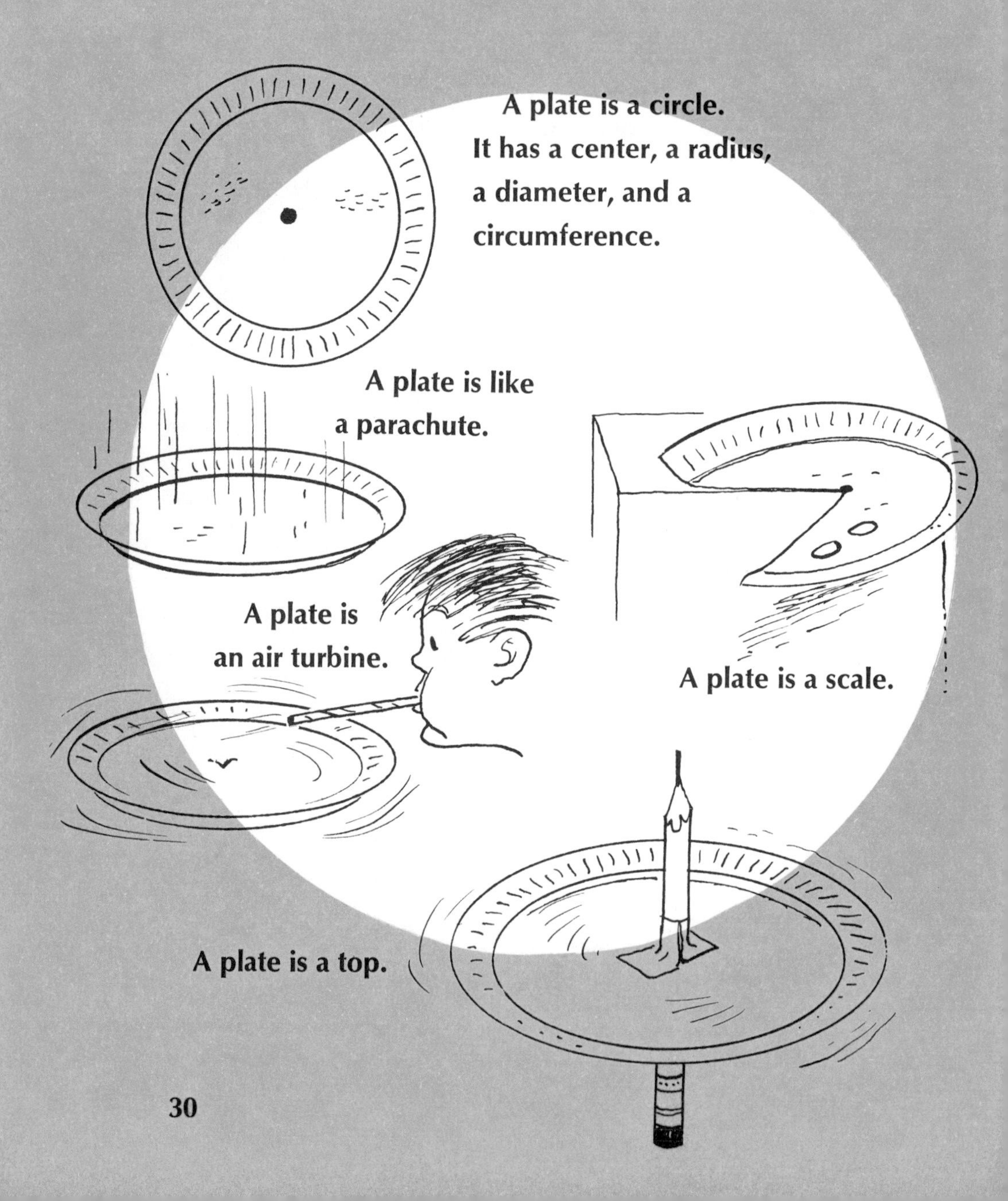

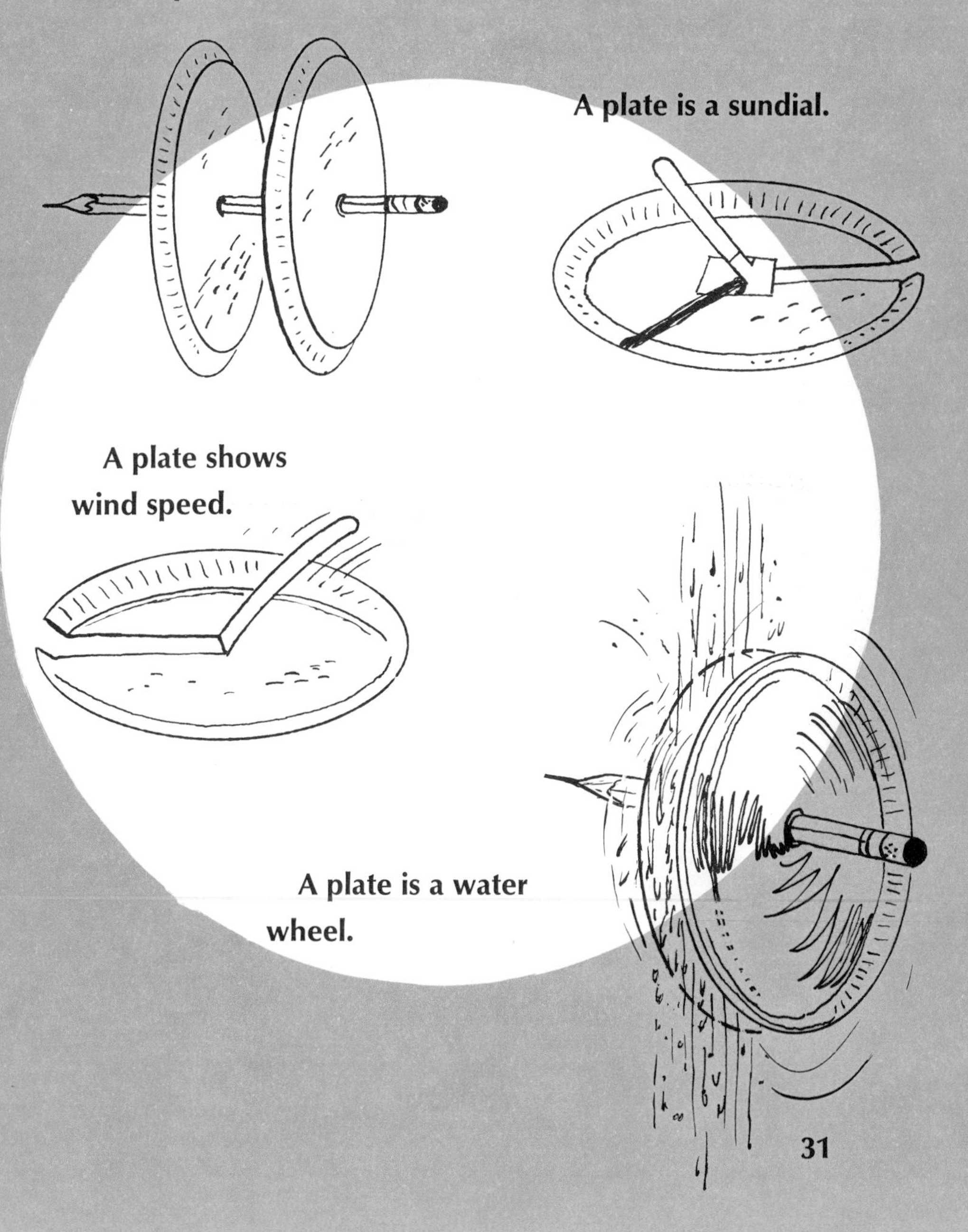
A plate is a wheel.
A plate is a sundial.
A plate shows wind speed.
A plate is a water wheel.

What else can you find out with a party plate?

Think of what you want to do.

Try it. See what YOU can discover.